Christian Poems

Composed By

Clement
Rajaratnam
Prabakaran

Copyright © 2014 by Clement Rajaratnam Prabakaran

Christian Poems
by Clement Rajaratnam Prabakaran

Printed in the United States of America

ISBN 9781628714784

All rights reserved solely by the author. The author guarantees all contents are original and do not infringe upon the legal rights of any other person or work. No part of this book may be reproduced in any form without the permission of the author. The views expressed in this book are not necessarily those of the publisher.

Unless otherwise indicated, the author used the Authorized or King James Version of the Bible.

www.xulonpress.com

To Dear
Nalanda, Prabahar
and children.

Best wishes
Love and Hugs

— Prabhu Anavan —

Foreword

It is my pleasure to commend this volume of poetry to you.

A lifetime of Clement R. Prabakaran's abiding spiritual depth shines through as he presents glimpses of the Christian faith in a way that is simple without being simplistic; as informative as they are comforting.

Christian Poems is refreshingly accessible to all ages, easily read with little ones at bedtime or by the fireside at prayer time. It can be enjoyed by those who have journeyed long in the tradition of Christianity and those for whom it may be a curiosity.

The Very Reverend Dr. S. Scott Hunter
Dean of the Cathedral Church of St. Paul, Detroit, Michigan
Epiphany 2014

Prologue

Poems are prose set to verse & rhyme.
I have expressed a two thousand year old guide for our life called BIBLE written in verse, set to rhyme.
The poems are short to keep our frail human attention span in focus. It helps adults in a hurry to skim and get the idea without details. I recommend the original (BIBLE) for that!
If children read this, all the more reason to keep this concise.
To put hundreds of years through human history into short poems from the BIBLE is an on-going effort.
This is a start.

DEDICATED TO:

My parents Alice & Richard Rajaratnam; and Siblings
My wife Prema Thangadurai for love & everything else.
My children who are precious; with my in-laws.
My grand-children who are loved and blessed.
Extended Family & Friends everywhere.

By: Clement Rajaratnam Prabakaran
    Sterling Heights, Michigan, USA.

Prologue Poem

I come before your presence
With thanksgiving and grateful heart.
You have shown me life's essence,
    A child of God set apart.
Give divine guidance to me
    Through daily life to death.
BIBLE spells **B-I-B-L-E**.
    Best **I**nstructions **B**efore **L**eaving **E**arth
Love God; Love neighbor;
Principles for good behavior.
    Be good to fellow beings,
    For God's choicest blessings.
With saints gone before,
Rest in peace evermore.

The B-I-B-L-E

The B-I-B-L-E is a acronym for "Best Instructions Before Leaving Earth".

The "BIBLE" can be looked upon as a Christian Guide through History. From the Old Testament foretelling Jesus Christ arrival to its New Testament Gospels of His arrival and His disciples witness, for us to follow.

The "Holy BIBLE" can be looked upon as God's literal Holy Word.

The Old Testament with its good and bad people, leaders, chosen people, wars, pestilence, and so on; to the New Testament with Jesus Christ Virgin birth as a Second Adam to absolve Humanity of original sin, conquer death by His resurrection and ascension, to the Holy Father's right hand.

Bibles come in different versions, since all were written by human beings guided by divine providence or otherwise; inclusive of all history or selectively edited to suit the times.

The following poems have been composed from and acknowledged through the Authorized or King James Version on its four hundredth anniversary on May 01, 2011.

The poems expressed are those of the writer alone and not intended to change, dispute or create discord among believers of the Holy Bible. If the poems are enjoyed and one soul turned to God, the mission is accomplished.

THE BIBLE

The BIBLE is eternal history of God.
    Old Testament foretelling arrival of Jireh Jehovah.
The Holy Bible is eternal word of God.
    New Testament; life, death and ascension of the Messiah.
From Adam and Eve @ the Garden of Eden,
To the Holy Temple City of Jerusalem.
    God's guidance to His chosen people,
    Through Jesus and his many a disciple.
Old starts with the creation of Man,
New ends with the Son of Man Revelation.
    Holy word spoken through the ages,
    Through Leaders, Judges, Prophets, Kings and Sages.
Best **I**nstructions **B**efore **L**eaving **E**arth,
We all know through BIBLE God careth.

BIBLE

This double edged sword
Contains God's Holy Word
    From the creation of the world
    To the life after in God's world
About you and me
Tells the B-I-B-L-E.
    Take it, read it and taste it
    To reach God bit by bit
To become a sinless Saint
Without the devilish taint
    The B-I-B-L-E
    Yes, that is the book for me
As a stepping stone to heaven
Is God's own Bible to us given

CREATION

In the beginning God moved around,
No sky, no earth, no water, no ground,
    Creating many things, many ways,
    All this in God's seven days.
Man to enjoy and co-exist with all.
Woman for company, before the fall.
    Fruits and Garden of Eden enjoyed they;
    Kicked out for they did not obey.
Earthly life was bestowed,
Time, talent and treasure endowed,
    Adam and Eve God created.
    Abel lived and Cain cheated.
God judged and Humans flourished,
Good and evil survived.

Adam and Eve

Beautiful Garden of Eden to enjoy,
Adam and Eve did resources employ.
    All creatures under their domain,
    Until serpent tempted the woman.
Original sin they did commit,
God's scheme of things they did not fit.
    From privilege to earthly life,
    Adam and Eve lived as man and wife.
Man to work, toil and sweat,
Woman to bear child in heat.
    All of us our sins, our burden,
    Humans ended up downtrodden.
To save us from original sin,
Later God sent His only begotten Son.

Adam & Eve

Adam & Eve
First people to live
With God in paradise
With exuberant ease
    Sinned against God
    That same patient Lord
    Sent them to this world
    Then an untidy mold
The wily devil snake
To Eve first spoke
And tempted the woman
Who tempted the man
    A certain fruit
    Told the devil brute
    Would turn a human
    To a God – Amen
Thus tempted
They ate quite contended
Which introduced sin
Like odor from a dustbin
    Sent out of paradise
    They roamed earth like two blind mice
    And that is how sin came
    With all its shame
Though they are our parents of old
We need not be in their hold
But turning away from sin
Enter God's heavenly inn.

Cain and Abel

Descendants of Adam and Eve,
Mark on this earth they did leave.
    Cain – tilled the ground to grow,
    Abel – hunting skills he did know.
Asked to show fruits of their livelihood,
Both brought forth the fruits to God.
    Cain brought bad, Abel brought good,
    Abel was blessed and Cain dismissed.
Cain was jealous and he sinned,
Brother Abel by Cain's hand was killed.
    "Am I my brother's keeper", he famously lied,
    And was marked with a curse on his head.
Early creatures of God Supreme,
Were a disappointment for His divine dream.

Noah Family

Future generations God created,
Giant men and women, human's begatted.
    Vile people they became;
    Noah family – only people sane.
God made Noah make an ark of gopher wood,
300 cubits long, 50 cubits wide, 30 cubits high; it stood.
    God organized creatures two by two inside,
    Man and mammals for eternity saved.
Forty days and forty nights of rain,
Wiped out humanity, except Noah name.
    Imagine Noah starting from scratch,
    A whole new human batch,
God made covenant with humans,
A rainbow to save future generations.

Tower of Babel

God saved Noah from flood, with sons.
And from root of Shem came nations,
    Lived in a land called Shi'-nar.
Speaking a common language sublime,
    Decided to build a city and tower,
With brick for stone and mortar of slime,
    To heaven they wanted to reach.
As God came down to visit,
    Decided a lesson for them to teach,
Confound their language he could not resist.
    Shem's children could not communicate,
    Babel of tongues did disseminate,
God scattered them far and abroad,
Humans with dialects did everywhere spread.

Abram and Sarai

Among the population and growth,
Through Noah and sons Shem, Ham, Japheth
    God chose nomad called Abram,
    Uprooted to give him land of Canaan.
His wife Sarai was barren;
Abram's name and inheritance was forsaken.
    A handmaid begat son Ishmael,
    But jealously banished them out on a trail.
As Abram flourished and settled in his tent,
And entertained three strangers that God sent.
    Wife Sarai was blessed for their charity.
    A son Isaac in old age – a rarity.
Abram and Sarai; God anointing,
Isaac was his father's blessing.
    When asked Isaac as a sacrifice,
    Abram did not think twice.
God blessed Abram's obedience,
With wealth and his sustenance.
    From Isaac his seed grew a nation,
    Forefather of many a generation.

ABRAHAM

Blessed Abram fortunes grew,
Kith and kin abundance knew.
    God renamed them Abraham and Sarah,
    Saved them from Sodom and Gomorrah.
Son Isaac had an arranged bride,
Cousin Rebecca from his mother's side.
    Though Abraham and Sarah lived a long and fruitful life,
    When God called, it was for the family, grief.
God blessed patriarch Abraham face to face,
A unique person of the human race.

Isaac

Only son of Sarah and patriarch Abraham,
Flourished under God's program.
    Searched by a loyal servant who said,
"This thing proceedeth from the Lord".
    Married cousin Rebecca as arranged.
God blessed Isaac and Rebecca well,
Under God's guidance they did dwell,
    Two sons Esau and Jacob were theirs.
    Father and Mothers favorites they vied as heirs.
Jacob tricked Esau's inheritance,
Took advantage of bad circumstance.
    Mother got Jacob the father's blessing,
    First born stature went trading.
Isaac was very old when he died,
Blessed as patriarch Abraham's seed.

Esau and Jacob

Two sons of Rebecca and Isaac,
Their rivalry for father's affection is classic.
    Older one sold inheritance for food,
    Younger one duped brother for blessings good.
One was mother's favorite son,
Father favored the older one.
    Jacob ran away to save his own life.
    Worked fourteen years for a favorite wife.
Duped by mother's brother Laban,
Worked hard and fortune did gain.
    Came back home to reconcile,
    With Esau who was by then docile.
Sons and grandsons of Abraham's seed,
Blessed by God indeed.

Jacob Israel

Jacob twelve sons made up Israel,
Descendants that went far and wide for real.
    Two from Rachel and six from Leah;
    Two each from Bilhah and Zilpah;
Israel's vast empire by son's created,
Hierarchy, and favorites by Jacob treated.
    The last two were Jacob's favorite,
    Joseph and Benjamin by brotherly rite.
Joseph got a multi-color coat,
Benjamin held on to his father's clout,
    Sent to get his brothers back home,
    Brothers sold him to strangers from out of town.
Hence the families and tribes of Israel,
From Canaan to Egypt did settle.

ISRAEL – JACOB

Grandson of a famous patriarch Abraham,
All through life had a grand program.
    Ran for his life from brother Esau's anger;
    Tricked father Isaac to be blessed from danger;
Worked hard and long years for his favorite wife.
Reconciled with family to start a new life,
    Along the way he stopped to dream at a well,
    Fought with God; for Him to dwell.
Established twelve tribes through sons as heirs,
Israel was the heritage given as theirs.
    Lived to see his sons blessed by God,
    As many tribes of Israel abroad,
Abraham's seed creating a nation,
Jacob Israel blessed as God's creation.

Joseph

Israel's tribes to Egypt sold Joseph.
Brothers told father that Joseph was messed up.
    Joseph worked in Pharaoh's court well,
With favor and riches, God blessed him.
    But jealousy put him in prison hell.
Joseph had a talent to decipher dream,
    Pharaoh's bad dream he interpreted good,
Made the Egyptian land get through famine.
    People came far and wide for food.
Israel sent sons to Egypt for their grain.
    Joseph toyed with them to see Benjamin,
    And reconciled with family again.
Israel's and Joseph's generations grew in Egypt,
Till slaves they became and sadly wept.

EGYPT

The Pharaoh dynasty on the river Nile,
Ruled with iron fist and merciless guile.
    Ramses built cities and monuments,
    With Israelite slaves and instruments.
But Israelite seed multiplied and grew,
Goshen and slavery is all they knew.
    Pharaoh killed any new Messiah child,
    As challenge to Egyptian rule so wild.
Moses mother put him in a reed basket to float,
A princess found him, as her own to gloat.
    Raised as a future Pharaoh successor,
    Moses saw Israelite people toil and suffer.
Finding his roots confused and terrified him,
To save Israelites whose lives were too grim.
    Discovered as an Egyptian with Israelite ties,
    Moses was banished into the desert as the bird flies.

Joseph

Jacob worked long years for uncle Laban,
    Falling in love with cousin Rachel,
Loved her two sons Joseph and Benjamin,
    Until Joseph was sold toward Egypt's trail.
Found favor with Pharaoh for a good life,
But betrayed by the same Pharaoh's wife,
    Put in prison and had family dreams,
    Interpreted butcher and baker's dreams.
He analyzed dreams and found Pharaoh's favor again,
Helped Egyptians during their lean famine time.
    Brothers came for help and unknowingly for food bargain,
    Recognized, and toyed with them for their crime,
Reunited with family and father Israel,
Prospered and in Egypt long did dwell.
Died and buried in Egypt for a long time,
Was brought by fleeing Israelites and interned in Shekhem.

Passover

Israel in Egypt under Pharaoh bondage,
From Joseph generation and age to age.
    Till Moses by God ordained independence to gain,
    To land of milk and honey; to land of Canaan.
Pharaoh steel heart brought plagues galore,
Hail, fire, locusts, first born death and more.
    God told Moses to have a solemn feast,
As death and destruction did passover.
    Egyptians lost their first born and beast,
Israelites under lamb's blood did take cover.
    Pharaoh knew who was God with might,
    No more plagues he could stand or fight.
From Goshen; from Egypt, they fled;
God and Moses, after Passover, the Israelites led.

Moses

Banished to the desert under the sun,
Moses survives to the land of Median.
    Tends flock for Jethro; with Sephora, settles down.
    But God calls him from a burning bush fully grown,
Tells him to lead Israel to freedom;
By God of all people, the Great I AM.
    With his desert staff and Aaron to agree,
    Moses visits Pharaoh to let Israelites free.
Hardened Pharaoh reneges on his promise,
Plagues are showered for his transgressions,
    First borns die before Pharaoh could relent,
    With full freedom the Israelites are sent.
Moses gathers his people and tribes,
To lead them where milk and honey flows.

Desert Days

Moses, Aaron, Joshua and the tribes of Israel,
Out of Egypt set forth on freedom trail.
    Pharaoh army followed in hot pursuit,
    Moses with his staff the Red Sea did part.
Tribes of Israel safely cross the sea,
Pharaoh pursuit ended as dead as can be.
    God guided Israel in the desert days,
    Through shortages of essentials in many ways.
A pillar of cloud by day without fright,
A pillar of fire by night for light,
    God provided manna for His people,
    But all the Israelites did was grumble.
Twice God gave people rules to follow,
Commandments for Israelites that often rang hollow.
    Moses could not take their groan,
    For forty years the desert they roam.
Aaron and Moses did not reach the Promised Land,
Milk and honey was not for them as planned.

Land of Israel

Israel in the Promised Land,
    Consolidated through divine providence,
Led by God calling His hand;
    Prospered through God's abundance,
Judges, prophets and leaders untold,
Kept the faithful in God's fold.
    Ruled through instructions by Jehovah-Jireh,
    Commandments and the Ark held high,
People lived through war and peace,
Humbled in defeat, victory with grace.
    To keep rule of law and peace,
    God put His anointed in place,
Judges, prophets, leaders made Israel,
God's chosen people.

JOSHUA

Joshua, son of Nun, took over from Moses and Aaron,
Fought many battles in lands barren.
    Israel sought the Promised Land,
    Fought other tribes for it, hand in hand.
A stumbling block – City called Jericho,
Fell to the sound of trumpets and their echo.
    Ark of the Covenant led the Israelites,
    Through their journey, fighting through sin and mess,
    Israel came to rest with plenty of money,
In Promised Land of milk and honey.
    Chosen people, seed of Abraham,
    Isaac, Jacob, Joseph, Moses and Aaron,
Through Joshua and God's guidance,
Eternal blessings of God's abundance.

Prophets

God lead His chosen peoples,
Through patriarchs, leaders, prophets, Angels,
    Patriarch Abraham, Leader Moses–and major Prophets;
    Elijah, Elisha, Isaiah, Jeremiah, Ezekiel – and Minor Prophets
Micah, Hosea, Joel, Amos and Obadiah,
Nahum, Habakkuk, and Zephaniah,
    Haggai, Zechariah, Malachi and others;
    Foretelling all what our life gathers.
Tempted and tested Job or a resurgent Daniel.
Repentant Jonah from the belly of a big fish–whale?
    Chosen people; but rebellious children,
    Created by God and banished from a Garden.
Prophets encompassed in a second Adam,
Jesus Christ, The Prophet; guide us to Father's heaven.

Samuel

A humble married woman named Hannah,
Prayed mumbling to God for a little manna.
    At the Temple, she prayed for a son,
    Priest at her mumbling thought she was on rum.
God heard her insistent prayers, and soon,
Unto her a dutiful son was given.
    Dedicated at the Temple to God,
    Samuel was given in favor, all good.
A learned prophet he turned out to be,
God's holy powers in him many did see.
    Counselor to kings Saul and David,
    Pointing out good and bad things they did.
God's anointed—a simple woman's request,
In Bible, as a major prophet, Samuel exists.

Isaiah

Isaiah; son of Amoz lived,
Under kings of Judah and believed,
    God's vision for His chosen people.
    God's mercy for Israel through His disciple,
Foretold the coming of the New Messiah,
Branch and stem of Jesse; Lord Jeho-vah.
    For unto us a Son is born,
    Prince of peace through a virgin.
Strength and my song; My salvation,
Wolf dwell with lamb; calf with lion.
    Sixty-six chapters of Isaiah vision,
    A guide to follow his direction.
Through Joseph dreams; Judah kings; Amoz shoot,
God's word spoken through Isaiah's root.

King Saul

God led the land and people of Israel,
Through prophets who served Him well.
    Brought them to a land of plenty,
    Land flowing with milk and honey,
A firm ruler the people needed,
An anointed king for Israel required.
    God told the prophet Samuel,
    To anoint Saul, king of Israel.
An able king to honor God,
Israel's teeming people he led.
    God blessed His new anointed king,
    With guidance only He could bring,
Till Saul forgot God's blessed choice,
Saul in his own power did rejoice;
    With power and sin Saul fell from grace,
    God's wrath he could not face.

King David

God's wrath against King Saul,
Made Him order prophet Samuel;
    To go find a replacement king,
    In the lineage of Abraham's seedling.
Son of Bethlehemite – Jesse; was youngest David.
Father's sheep take care of, he did;
    Fighting beasts like lions,
    Goliath and the Philistines.
Samuel was sent to anoint;
King of Israel God did appoint,
    Young David to rule,
    God's chosen Jewish people.
With God and prophets as guide,
Ruled in war and peace; King David.

King Solomon

King David had many a son,
But God selected His favorite one.
    Young, but mature was Solomon,
    Ambitions for power and wealth he had none,
To rule he asked God wisdom,
As he inherited David's vast kingdom.
    God showered that with many other things,
    Judged Solomon over all his beings.
Gave true mother her contested child,
Queen of Sheba and Pharaoh's child,
    Other queens and kings visited him with awe;
    Through Proverbs and Songs of Solomon he showered love,
Built a great Temple for praise of God,
Jerusalem became center of the Hebrew world.

Samson

Samson was a strong Nazarite,
    Born of Zorah Danites Manoah; a son.
Was endowed with power and might,
    Out of prayer through an Angel given.
Tribe that fought the Philistines,
Ripped jaw bones from tribe of lions.
    No razor touched his tousled head,
    Cutting hair would his strength shed.
To Delilah; his love, Samson had sworn.
Enemies wanted his secret strength known;
    Delilah tricked him thrice to find,
    Where his strength lay in kind.
She cut his hair; he lost his might;
Philistines tortured; put out his sight;
    Samson grew hair; found his strength back.
From prison he escaped to find the Temple,
    Finding two columns; Philistines he did attack,
Destroyed Philistines; died, but saved Israel.

JEREMIAH

This son of Hiekiah,
    In the land of Benjamin.
Wrote Lamentations – This Jeremiah.
    Under Neb-u-chad-nez-zar; king of Babylon,
Chaldean seventh year captivity of Israel,
For deserting true God in lieu of Baal,
    Found God @ hand; God of righteousness.
    God; separator of good figs & bad figs.
Jeremiah prophesized for kings of Judah,
Jehoi-a-kim or Josiah or son Zedekiah.
    With prophet Micah, the Mo-ras-thite,
    Lead Israel through peace and fight.
Chosen people this prophet did need,
For kings blessed by God to be led.

Jonah

God directed His chosen prophet Jonah,
    From Hebrew land, and son of A-mit'-tai.
To go save the people of Nin'-e'veh',
    People gone astray with loose ends to tie.
But our disobedient prophet Jonah,
Went by sea to Tarsish and to Joppa.
    God's anger turned into a storm,
    Making ship folk scared and squirm.
They cast lots for a sacrifice to sea,
Which fell on Jonah; who this did not foresee.
    A great fish swallowed our Jonah whole,
    Three days, three nights, (we assume inside a whale?).
Prayed; as God made great fish vomit,
Jonah went and made Nin-e'-veh' commit.
    Jonah saw his purpose @ Nin-e'-veh',
    Repentant people praising God Jir-o-veh.

DANIEL

Daniel lived in Je-hoi-akim, a Judah fiefdom,
Under a Neb-u-chad-nez-zar ruled kingdom.
    Daniel was a skillful male, cunning in knowledge,
    Understanding science, wisdom, and raised in privilege.
Daniel (And Han-a-ni-ah; Mi-sha-el ; Az-a-ri-ah),
Interpreted king's dreams through master Ar-i-och.
    Renamed Bel-te-shaz-zar, Shadrach and Abed – ne-go,
    Refused to worship graven Chaldean images with a 'No'.
Thrown into a burning fiery furnace to die,
An Angel joined them to keep the three alive.
    Promoted by Cyrus the Persian successor king,
    Daniel was thrown to lions by Darius the new king.
Safely protected by God and freed by Darius,
Daniel foretold end of days and prayed for people's peace.

Psalms

Son of Jesse; a young unknown shepherd,
Out among sheep in wilderness, he often heard,
    God and nature to him talking.
    Though wolves and lions were stalking,
David's harp poured out his heart,
Some praise; some sad; some with mirth,
    Blessing a man who fears God,
    Or confess 'Lord is My Shepherd'.
A prayer for confession, mercy and strength,
A prayer for refuge, help and God's breath,
    Lifting eyes unto the high hills for God;
    Long life and blessing through His word;
One fifty Psalms did young David write,
Reading them makes one's life a little brite.

APOCRYPHA

The hidden books of the Holy BIBLE.
    Special grouping from 'Esdras' to 'Maccabees',
Deemed by some forefathers as not likeable.
    Removed 'Judith' from BIBLE so no one sees,
From '1 & 2 Esdras' to '1 & 2 Maccabees';
From 'Tobit' or 'Prayer of Mannases';
    'Rest of Esther' or Solomon's 'Wisdom';
    Daniel's 'Song of the Three Children';
'Baruch' and the 'Epistle of Jeremy', or;
'Story of Susanna' nobody cared for.
    The idol 'Bel & the Dragon Book',
    Did not deserve a second look.
'Apocrypha' deleted from the BIBLE,
Will not matter as food for our soul.

Old Testament

From our original parents Eve and Adam,
Came to earth, Son of Man.
    Man survived Noah flood days,
    God chose Abraham many ways,
Isaac; and Jacob blessed as Israel,
Joseph; Moses led slaves out as free people.
    Joshua found the Promised Land,
    Of milk and honey through God's guiding hand.
Judges, Prophets, Priests, led,
And kept Israelite people fed.
    Saul and King David were chosen ahead,
    By God and Samuel their people to lead.
God choses people in His time,
Great Jehovah – Jireh; the Great 'I AM'.

New Testament

Foretold by Prophet Isaiah,
Reiterated by Prophet Micah,
    A second Adam to earth did come.
    To take out our sins and then some.
Virgin birth in a humble manger,
Survived Herod, temptation, wrath and danger.
    Preached; love God, love neighbor,
    Rules for human good behavior.
Life of Christ in four Gospels,
Other gospels by unofficial disciples,
    Paul's letters; Acts; Peter; John's Revelation,
    New Testament of God's incarnation.
Perfect complement of Old Testament history,
New Testament reveals Father, Son & Spirit's Glory.

Ten Commandments

Ten Commandments God did give,
    To Moses in a desert as a guide.
Rules to be good enough and humbly live,
    To get us safely on God's side.
Thou shalt honor the Great 'I AM' God.
No other idols before Almighty Lord.
    Honor father and mother for long life,
    No adultery – to honor spouse or wife,
No killing; no coveting things of neighbor,
From temptations and sins; God to deliver.
    Jesus took the ancient tablets from Father,
    And simply said, "Love God, love neighbor".
Including all the laws and prophets guide,
To get us all to His Father's heavenly side.

Jesus Birth

In the lineage of King David,
A second Jo'seph came ahead.
    A humble young handmaiden, Mary,
    Virgin though; God's seed did carry.
Accepted by Jo'seph, Mary visits Elizabeth,
Ordered by Romans, they leave Nazareth.
    O little town of Bethlehem,
    Blessed manger where Jesus was born,
Shepherds came by to wonder and adore,
Wise men duped Herod and followed a star.
    Parents wondered about this God child,
    Herod got scared and had children killed,
To safety of Egypt Jo'seph family fled,
Came back to Nazareth and lived.

A Christmas Poem

Christmas is a celebration.
    The birth of Jesus Christ.
Celebrated by many a nation,
    His birth through Virgin Mary; a first.

Christmas is a birthday.
Baby laid in a manger with hay,
    Celebrated not like any birthday of us,
    But humbly by shepherds, kings and prophets.

Christmas is a festival.
    A baby's birth from God to us,
To be good and conquer evil,
    To take our sins later to His cross.

Christmas is a tradition.
    Santa, tree, parties, and carols,
Christmas is God's rendition,
    Of Son Jesus, through saints and angels.

Christmas is a reminder.
Every year with its grandeur,
    God's gift of a Child Savior,
    To keep us blessed with peace and good behavior.

Christmas is a greeting.
    "Merry Christmas" to all; we bless,
A Happy New Year also we ring,
    For God to be with all of us.

Jesus Youth

Mary and Jo'seph settled down in Nazareth,
Following traditional Jewish faith.
    Jesus grew up as a carpenter's son,
    With relatives like cousin John.
Went to Jerusalem Temple festival,
Pondered scriptures with sages at a high level,
    Parents got worried and searched for Him,
    Found Him three days later having Godly fun.
Starting divine Father's business then,
Earthly parents wondered about Him,
    As mother Mary kept Him in her heart,
Jesus grew up in wisdom and stature.
    God's work Jesus did start,
In favor with God and Man to mature.

First Miracle

God made man and woman,
Woman Eve and man Adam.
    Set them in the Garden of Eden,
    A marriage of sorts in Heaven.
Jesus got an invitation,
    To a Cana wedding, by the groom.
Among the mirth and celebration,
    Wine ran out in the room.
Mother Mary alerted Jesus,
Who did not care much about the fuss.
    Jesus told stewards to fill jars with water,
    And serve them when needed later.
Water turned to sweet wine; loved by host and disciples,
Marriage sanctified by Jesus first of many miracles.

GOSPELS

Gospel means "Good News".
    Four of them in the Bible hold.
We hear them read from Church pews.
    Matthew, Mark, Luke and John; Jesus life told;
Matthew; the longest from genealogy and conception,
To birth, life, death and resurrection.
    Mark; the shortest hit ground running,
    From baptism, life, death, ascension, praising.
Luke; the physician with other details similar,
Jesus birth, life, teachings we are familiar.
    John incarnates Jesus as Lord,
    Father and Son in one accord.
Synoptic gospels are the first three;
Canonical gospel was John's entrée.

John the Baptist

Dedicated at the Temple as a child,
    Jesus came to John at the river Jordan.
To be baptized, humble and mild,
    Blessed by Father God in heaven.
A dove descended to witness,
Father's pleasure in Son's greatness.
    Cousin John humble life style,
    Honey and locusts is not a life lived well.
John accused the king of mistakes,
Lost his head and life for higher stakes.
    Jesus felt for His cousin's life,
    Jesus felt His own future grief,
Started his father's mission with miracles,
Selected twelve cherished disciples.

ACTS

In the Roman lineage came Saul,
Converted in a miracle, to Paul.
    Documents Acts of the Apostles,
    Recounting Jesus life with His disciples.
Ordaining Matthi'-as, Joseph Bar'-sa-bus Justus,
Peter, john gathering leaders and hosts.
    Story of Stephen the first martyr,
    Saul had a hand in this disaster.
Traveled the then known Roman world,
Brought other faithful to god's fold.
    Disciples receive Pentecost blessing,
    Jesus good news far and wide spreading,
Father's guidance, from acts of apostles to Paul,
Put Christianity on the world for the long haul.

St. Paul

Saul – A citizen of Rome,
Persecuted Christians all over and then some.
    Till God revealed in a Road to Damascus dream,
    Having received many a martyr's scream.
Converted to Paul and the good side,
Christian faith then he could not hide.
    Wrote a treatise to The-oph-ilus.
    From selecting Judas replacement Matthi-us,
To revealing Christ life history,
And early Apostles witness story.
    A book on the Acts of the Apostles,
    First martyr Steven; to become a disciple,
Saul the Roman to Apostle Paul he converted,
Many a life to Christ Jesus he turned.

ST. PETER

Simon – brother of Andrew and son of Jonah,
Came from the town of Beth-sa-i-da.
   A raw cut, toiling, simple fisherman,
   Christ turned him into fishers of men.
By Jesus side, but ignorant of greatness,
Mother-in-law's health and other miracles did witness.
   Tried to walk on water on a dare,
   Acknowledged Jesus as his savior.
Went to top of Jesus mountain,
God's purpose for Jesus he could not ascertain.
   Wanted whole body washed by Jesus,
   Time of trial denied Jesus, but did confess.
On this brazen raw cut fisher man same,
Rock, roots and seeds of Christianity came.

In God's time

First miracle in Cana our Lord Jesus did,
After His hour is not come, He said.
    A blind man from his birth cured,
    So god's glory through Jesus revealed.
A palsied man by the Angels pool waiting,
Jesus made him well to take up is bedding.
    His strength drained when garment touched,
    By a trembling woman to be eternally blessed.
Ten lepers shunned by a lofty society,
Cured; with only one to thank his savior deity.
    Jairus daughter, Centurion's servant ill,
    Demonic man exorcised for pigs to kill,
Lazarus and a mother's only son raised again,
God's glory to shine; in God's due time.
    Salvation comes to those who wait,
    God takes care of us from Satan's bait.

Holy Week

Jesus Christ rode a donkey to Jerusalem;
Rode in majesty on a bed of palm.
    Went to temple and merchants scatter,
    Holy place for sellers; did not matter.
Had a last supper; communion and served,
Told disciples of brooding times ahead.
    Went to Gethsemane Garden to pray,
    Judas found him to betray.
Soldiers took him like a thief and coward,
Jesus healed a servant's ear cut by a sword,
    Mock trial by Pilate, Scribes, Pharisees,
    Led Him to the stations of the cross.
Crowned and crucified as a third thief,
From sin as savior He gave us relief.

CRUCIFIXION

Son of Man came down from Heaven,
For our original sin and earthly misbehaving.
    Jewish elders turned Jesus in,
    Roman rulers did not care for Him.
Crucifixion on a wooden cross;
Was Roman punishment to repress.
    Pilate washed off his hand,
    Disciples feared enough to disband,
Hung between two convicts bad,
A crown of thorns Jesus had.
    Few statements in pain He made,
    Mother, convert, thirst, Father 'forgive', He said,
Jesus gave up His life for us,
Descended to hell and deep abyss.

A poem for Lent

    Forty days and forty nights.
Son of Man spent in penitence,
Son of Man with a lot of patience.
        Us frail humans He came to save,
        We frail humans who misbehave.
Oh, the Passion of the Christ;
Who for us suffered hunger and thirst.
    Forty days and forty nights.
Satan's temptation He did resist,
For all the sins we must also detest.
        Original sin of Adam and Eve,
        And our sins He did receive.
Our cross He carried up a hill,
As Romans put Him through a crucifixion drill.
    Forty days and forty nights.
The season of penitential Lent,
Son of Man by God was sent.
        He died on the cross for us,
        Carrying our sins to death's abyss.
God so loved the world He created,
His Son victorious, as Satan retreated.
    Forty days and forty nights.
We should follow Christ example too,
Simple acts of faith to do.
        Love God and love neighbor,
        Resisting Satan altogether.
Death and Satan through faith vanquished,
Our sins and earthly life all finished.
    Forty days and forty nights.
    God has us in His sight.
So on that glorious resurrection Easter Day,
With praise and thanks to God we pray.

LENT AND EASTER

Forty days; not counting Sundays, from Lent to Easter;
Jesus penanced for Man's worldly disaster.
    Lent is a time for our penance from sin,
      And at Easter resurrection morning, new life begin.
Easter is always on a Sunday;
    Following the first full moon;
After the vernal equinox day;
    The date never too late or too soon,
Occurs earliest in March twenty-second,
    Occurs latest on April Twenty-fifth.
Shrove Tuesday we stuff pancakes and paczki's to no end,
    Good Friday we fast to lessen our girth.
Holy week starts on Palm Sunday,
    As Jesus rode in majesty to Jerusalem.
Had His last supper and prayed on Maundy Thursday,
    To be betrayed by Judas and to be slain.
The trial was full of Roman injustice,
Good Friday they hung Jesus on a cross,
    Holy Saturday is set apart for our preparation,
    To seek Jesus after His resurrection.
"For God so loved the world that
He gave His only begotten Son that
    Whosoever believeth in Him should not perish
But have eternal life".
    Easter Sunday we celebrate and bless,
God's gift of that everlasting life.
    Any Easter relevance to a bunny,
    Is as far as the egg is to a bunny.

Lent to Easter

Forty days and forty nights,
    Is the season of Lent.
Christians give up some rights,
    To straighten out a life they bent.
Give up candy, give up cake,
    Alcohol, tobacco or meat they give up,
Hoping a better person it will make.
    Sincerely regret and never dupe,
Seven days a week we should be good.
Don't have to give up food,
    Don't use Lent as mid-course correction,
    Sundays are days of resurrection.
As at the end we gather,
    Giving up things ring hollow,
Love God and love neighbor,
    Jesus teachings try to follow.
Simple teaching, simple guide,
As life's ups and downs we ride.
    All through our lives we should,
    Live life the best we could.
Live a good Lent every day,
And look forward to Easter resurrection Sunday.

Resurrection

Christ died on the dross for our sins;
Was buried in a new tomb closed with stones.
    He descended into hell three days,
    Fought death and devil for us, many ways.
Suffering and pain of that fateful Friday,
Son of Man came on earth to save the day.
    As faithful women went to see,
    What Jesus death and burial may be,
No stone; no body; no death to worry.
Only bright Angels' Jesus to heaven to carry,
    Christ is risen, Alleluia, they were told.
    Disciples came to see & to behold,
Empty tomb to note the risen Christ,
From sin and death our freedom, with Alleluia burst.

Easter

God and Moses, the Israelites led,
From Egyptian slavery as they fled.
    That Jewish Old Testament of Passover,
    Led New Testament Christians to Lent and Easter.
Crucified Son of Man from grave did rise,
Paid with His blood our sins to suffice.
    On glorious resurrection day,
    Alleluias we sing and pray.
Easter symbol of a bunny,
Painted eggs; they are just as funny.
    Politically correct and generic they are,
    But true meaning of Easter they ignore.
Easter is a joyous season,
The risen Christ is the reason.
    Immanuel means "God with us",
    The risen Christ with us to bless.
Alleluia means, "All hail to Him who is",
Happy Easter; Alleluia we praise.

Ascension

As disciples and women left the grave confused,
Mary Magdalene to give up Jesus refused.
    Asked Jesus; assuming Him the gardener ,
    To give Jesus remains to her.
As Jesus revealed Himself in glory,
Rab-bo'-ni she called, relieved and happy.
    Doubting Thomas and some did not believe them,
    Till Jesus and others confirmed His resurrection.
Revealing Himself a few times to Apostles,
Jesus sent them to preach the Gospel.
    Ordained us all to reveal God's glory,
    Son of Man victory over sin; story.
Ascending and sitting with Father in Heaven,
Second Adam back to Garden of Eden.

Angels and Demons

The spirit of God moved upon the face of the waters,
As Angels designed the earth of our fathers.
    Adam and Eve in Eden broke God's holy word,
    Cher-u-bim guarded Eden with flaming sword.
Angel stopped Abram offering of Isaac his son,
At Je-ho-vah Ji-reh by God – the great 'I AM'.
    Two angels came and sat at the gate in Sodom City,
    Lot hosted them before God spared him with pity.
Jacob saw angels by ladder ascending and descending,
Fought with them at Beth-el to receive blessing.
    Sons of God and Satan presented themselves to God,
    To test Job who remained loyal to his Lord.
Daniel and friends in a fiery furnace with angels,
Daniel saved by Angels in a den of lions.
    Joshua resisted Satan standing before Angels,
    Ezekiel saw visions at Che'-bar of cher-u-bims.
God sent an Angel to select Mary with delight,
Righteous priest Zacharias questioned and Angel;
Till wife Elizabeth bore John as told by that angel Gabriel.
Angels announced Jesus birth to shepherds at night.
    Satan took Jesus over the world to tempt Him,
Jump off the temple and Angels will help he said,
Worship me for riches or turn stone into bread,
    Jesus overcame temptation as Angels served Him.
As Peter cut off a servant's ear at Jesus betrayal,
Jesus could have asked His Father a thousand Angels,
    Son of Man died for our sins and descended into hell,
    Rose again in three days to befit an Angel.
Satan hath desired to have and sift us like wheat,
But Angels from God keep us away from Satan's feet.

Twelve Disciples

Jesus chose twelve disciples,
Whom He could trust as Apostles.
   Simon Jonah, Jesus renamed him Peter,
   Andrew Jonah fisherman was his brother.
James and John Zeb'-e-dee; sons of thunder,
Brothers' bo-an-er'-ges; names you wonder!
   First four among equals, Jesus drew.
   From Bethsa'-i-da Philip and Andrew,
Bar-thol'-omeo, Thomas, thad-de'-us,
Mathew, and James son of Al-the'-us,
   Simon the Can'nnanite,
   Treasurer Judas Iscariot.
A band of brothers for Jesus Christ,
Love God, love neighbor, Jesus taught them first.

Followers

Jesus had many other followers;
Siblings Martha, Mary and Lazarus.
    Oh how our Lord loved these three;
    From death Lazarus, He did free.
Nathaniel; a man with no guile said Jesus,
Levi; tax collector and son of Al-phe'-us,
    Nicodemus a short learned Pharisee,
    Born again Christianity he did see.
Jesus ate with a cured Simon the leper,
From Mary's sin he did absolve her,
    Simon of Cy-re'-ne helped carry Jesus cross,
    Joseph of Ar-im-a-thea took Jesus down from the cross,
Mary Magdalene, Mary Zeb'-e-dee and the other Mary,
Jesus touched many lives in a hurry.

Church History

Kicked out of Garden of Eden,
Earthly bound were Adam and Eve.
    Noah's generation died in the great flood,
    Noah's family spared for being good.
Abraham obeyed God implicitly,
His seed blessed by God nicely.
    Moses got God's commandments ten,
    Roamed the desert in search of Canaan.
Through Judges and Sages God ruled Israel,
Mostly good people, but many did fail.
    Kind Saul, King David; settled down,
    King Solomon wore a wise crown,
Built a temple per God's plan,
A place to assemble and worship the great, 'I AM'.

CHURCHES

In the beginning the Spirit moved,
So how can we have God in a place tied?
    Cain and Abel gave burnt offerings,
    Abraham's altar was ready for Isaac's suffering.
Moses met God at a burning bush,
Aaron assembled golden calf in a rush.
    Even Solomon's temple of gold,
    Or Gothic Cathedrals or modern glass on wood,
No place of worship can God hold.
Yet we assemble to worship God,
    Away from sin to keep life simple,
    Your pure body and mine is God's temple.
Love God; love neighbor; said Jesus,
Worship anywhere; God will be with us.

PRIESTS

Priests are folks like you and me,
    Set apart, dedicated to lead people
Faithful to our Lord and Savior be,
    Like a chosen Jesus disciple,
Learn the Bible; learn theology,
Learn one holy Catholic Church ideology.
    Jesus has shown the way,
    To serve and be humble day by day.
Study and dedicate life to God first,
Bring people to our Savior Jesus Christ.
    Men and women of holy cloth do,
    Deserve our respect and support too.
As we journey through this perilous life,
To be saved from original sin and strife.

VERGERS

Verger carries a virge or a mace,
    To clear a path for priest or clergy.
All roads lead to a heavenly place,
    To praise God with a lot of energy.
Verger helps church service go well,
So God in our worship can dwell.
    Bless O' Lord the work Verger's do;
    All glory be to Trinity too.

The Sacraments

Ordained by God, snake crawls on its belly,
Ordained by God, woman carries a baby,
    Man works hard by the sweat of his brow,
    Woman holds a family to grow.
Baptism through rinsing by Holy water,
We are marked as Christ own forever.
    As we mature and get older,
    Christian vows we confirm and take over.
As woman to man; God gave to Adam; Eve.
As husband and wife together to live,
    Earthly worship of God we make.
    Creed, confession and absolution we take.
Jesus last supper, death and Resurrection,
Communion with Him is our remuneration.

Lord's Prayer

Disciples asked Jesus, 'how to pray',
A short gem for us all to say.
    "Our Father", it starts; to praise HIM,
    "Thy will be done" says Jesus, His Son.
Asks God for daily bread,
For food, shelter and clothing need.
    Asks God for forgiveness of sin,
    For us to forgive others for the same.
Asks God to block out temptation,
For us to stop evil & degradation.
    Confirms God's kingdom, power and glory,
    For ever and ever His "Great I AM" story.
An all-encompassing prayer for us,
Disciples request and a guide for us.

Teachings

Wise men at Jesus birth came to adore him,
    Jesus debated with sages at Temple of Jerusalem,
Jesus increased in God's wisdom,
    In favor with Father and Man.
Earthly father a carpenter of wood,
Divine Father set principles of good.
    Love God, love neighbor,
    Among commandments these two favor.
Beatitudes spelled out of God's fount.
    Worldly kingdom He did not want to rule,
    Eternal life for earthlings is more cool.
Adam and Eve and our original sin,
Destroyed for our new life to begin.

The Beatitudes

Blessed are the poor in spirit; for,
Theirs is the kingdom of heaven.
Blessed are the peacemakers; for,
They shall be called God's children.
Blessed are the meek; for,
They shall inherit the earth.
Blessed are they which do hunger and;
Thirst after righteousness; for,
They shall be filled to their girth.
Blessed are the pure in heart; for,
They shall see God.
Blessed are they that mourn; for,
They shall be comforted by the Lord.
Blessed are the merciful; for,
They shall obtain mercy.
Blessed are ye when men revile you and
Persecute you for My sake, falsely.
Blessed are they which are persecuted for
Righteousness sake,
For, theirs is the kingdom of heaven to take.
Rejoice and be glad;
Great is your heavenly reward.

Miracles

From the first miracle of Cana wedding,
To the last sword cut ear for healing,
    Jesus performed many miracles.
    A power He bestowed on His disciples.
Ten lepers cured & legions of demons removed.
Palsied man hand cured & blind men to see cured.
    Woman with a rare disease touched his garment and praised.
    Jairus daughter and Lazarus from death he raised.
A mother argued for crumbs from a table,
Jesus healed with compassion for all that He was able.
    Feeding four or five thousand was easy,
    Walk on water or stifle sea that was breezy.
Physical and worldly ailments Jesus did cure,
But preached love of God for heart's pure.

Book of Common Prayer

Read Bible to become knowledgeable.
Believe Bible to become unshakeable.
    Practice Bible to become righteous.
    Use Book of Common Prayer to become religious.
There is no line dividing either book,
    Bible is God's history and revelation.
Book of Common Prayer is for guidance we can look,
    Both we need for our holy consecration.
Prayers for everything the Book of Common Prayer contain,
Worship and grace at church service we attain.
    Baptism, confirmation, reception, communion,
    Marriage, healing, specials and reunion,
Book of Common Prayer guides our life through all,
So for Christ saving grace we may call.

Holy Communion

One of the Holy sacraments,
Apt for one's life compartments.
    Sharing Holy bread and wine,
    With Christ; last supper we dine.
Christ blessed bread as His body,
For us to take and be somebody.
    Christ blessed wine as His blood,
    For us to drink and behave good.
Doing this to remember Jesus Christ,
His goodness and mercy we thirst.
    Partaking meal with His disciples,
    Christ gave us His cherished principles.
"Love God and lovingly serve others",
Holy Communion – we in Him and Him in us.

Revelation

The Revelation of St. John the Apostle;
    Twenty-two visioned chapters from Isle of Patmos.
Greetings to seven churches in Asia from this disciple,
    Things John saw as a testimony to Jesus.
Seven candlesticks; tribes; books with seals;
    Seven thunders; trumpets; vials of wrath.
Seven stars; assured multitudes; and seven Angels.
    Michael's angels fighting red dragon breath;
Curse of the bad; fall of Babylon.
New heaven; new earth; New Jerusalem.
    Book of life lead to living waters,
    Satan beat and bound for a thousand years.
Potent visions through John, God did send,
The Alpha, Omega; the Beginning and the End.

Morning Prayer

Thank you Lord for a peaceful night.
Thank you Lord for sunshine bright.
    Fully rested and ready for the day,
    Lead us in your Holy path today.
May we meet peaceful neighbor folk,
To do your will, duty and work.
    Make us—love neighbor; love God,
    Through Jesus Christ our Savior Lord.

Evening Prayer

Thank you Lord for another blessed day,
With thanksgiving we come to pray.
    Be with us this night so dark,
    Next to us your guardian Angels park.
Counting blessings as we sleep,
Be with us, O Shepherd of your sheep.
    Bless us, rest us, wake us bright;
    Evermore with your guiding light.

Daily Bread

Jesus prayed: "Give us our daily bread".
Thank you Lord for keeping us fed.
    For us, more than we can count to date ,
    Remember those who have less on their plate.
For bountiful blessings given to us,
Thank you Lord and Savior Jesus.
    Give us love and faith to grow,
    Be with us and dear ones now.

TRAVEL PRAYER

Lord who sent Abraham to a new land,
Lord who sent Moses to the Promised Land,
    Lord who sent Paul across Roman land,
    Lord who sent Apostles all over Holy Land.
Send us out to travel in Safety,
Send us Angels to guide us safely,
    Send us Patron St. Joseph to be with us,
    Send with us your Son, our Savior Jesus.

Amen

The most common word in any prayer;
Christians end with an 'Amen' as they gather.
    "So be it" is what it means,
    Lord's Prayer, or your requested dreams.
"Our Father . . ." started Jesus, teaching us to pray;
"Amen" he concluded the prayer, His way.
    "So be it" echo our wishes; to God.
    For heavenly grace or earthly goods; to God.
We end our church prayers in Amen song,
Single fold, three, five or seven fold long.
    Careful what you wish for, as we with Amen end;
    "So be it" will God with grace respond.
Paul says, "For him and through him and to him,
Are all things; to whom be glory forever. Amen".

Alleluia

"Alleluia" we sing to God in praise,
Meaning, "All hail to Him who is".
    Sung mostly during Eastertide,
    We see Jesus resurrected to Father's side.
Omitting Alleluias during Lenten days,
We confess our sinful human ways.
    As we worship the great I AM,
    Father, Son and Holy Ghost before Abraham.
"Alleluia, Jesus Christ is risen" we greet,
"The Lord is risen indeed", we responsively tweet.
    Hosannas we sing to praise God,
    Death defeated by an Almighty God,
Give Alleluias due for our Savior Jesus,
"All hail to Him who is".

TRINITY

Trinity is Father, Son and Holy Ghost,
God, Jesus; One as Heavenly Host.
    Satan did acknowledge Jesus as divine;
    Tempting God to commit sin.
Original Adam in the image of God,
Fell from grace as Eve and serpent did.
    Original sin engraved in human kind,
    Second Adam to save our human behind.
God sent Jesus His blessed Son,
Jesus said, 'Me and my Father are one'.
    Jesus crucified to save us and conquer death,
    Ascended to Father as Spirit of eternal breath.
Trinity is God, Jesus, one Holy Ghost.
Alpha, Omega, the first and the last.

God's Commandment

Laws of the ancient Judeo tradition,
To keep humanity from perdition.
    Some six hundred plus per learned scholars;
    Too much for faithful wearing collars and us.
God simplified them to ten, as His commandment;
Moses placed it in the Ark of the Covenant.
    Sadducees who were silenced by Jesus,
    Sent lawyers for the other Pharisees;
Asked Him for the greatest commandment,
To see if legally Jesus would Moses law, dissent.
    "Love God with all your heart, soul and mind",
    "Love neighbor as thyself in anyone you find".
Two simple laws to love and follow, said Jesus,
To lead us to God in heaven above us.

CHRIST

The thing called life,
Anatomized by a knife.
    Reveals a sad state,
    Joy it away does take,
To make a human mad,
Depressed and bad.
    But the deity called Christ,
    Quenches your troubled thirst.
Christ if you believe,
I am sure he will you relieve,
    From the worldly crutches,
    And the devil's clutches.
Crises never aggravate,
For you at heaven's gate,
    Christ if you trust,
    You are His guest.

CHRISTIANS

In the beginning God created Adam and Eve.
First Christians made by God and Father, as humans to be.
    Whether Noah from a flood and humanity risen;
    Or Abram seed through only son Isaac was chosen.
An entire nation in the Jewish tradition as holy,
Moses led them to Canaan land of milk and honey.
    Kings Saul, David, Solomon were led and followed God;
    Till they fell from grace by the evil ways they trod.
Prophets foretold a Son to the world come to save us,
A humble child grown full of patience, love and grace.
    Chosen Christians by God are many in the Bible;
    Chosen Son of God came to live as one of us, and gullible.
Love God, love neighbor; Christ preaching never rings hollow;
For Christians; as followers of Christ, a commandment to follow.

THE CROSS

A Latin "Cruz" or Cross is a geometric figure; two lines perpendicular at best;
Covering our body and soul; up and down–North & South; sideways–West & East.
Deuteronomy mentions death by execution for crimes, on a tree.
    Ancient Egyptians had an 'Ankh'; not for death, but for life and fertility.
Roman scourge of crucifixion for death by execution for crimes, its enemies did hate.
Romans hung all martyrs on Appian Way or condemned them outside Esquiline Gate.
    A condemned death by Romans meant humiliation and execution;
    Our Lord and Savior Jesus Christ suffered on our behalf, that crucifixion.
Apostle Peter was hung upside down on the cross unworthy & unlike Christ, to suffer and die;
Apostle Andrew was hung 'X' unworthy & unlike Christ, to suffer and die.
    King Constantine embraced Christianity and finally abolished the crucifixion horror;
    For Cross as a symbol with the dove, fish, shepherd crook and anchor.
A Cross with INRI to proclaim Jesus Christ 'King of the Jews'.
In faith, prayer and Amen – as followers of Christ, the Cross guides us.

TALK TO GOD

God talked to Adam in Garden of Eden,
God talked about Abel to Cain,
    God talked to Noah about the great flood,
    God talked to Abram for his chosen good.
Jacob wrestled with God in a dream,
Joseph interpreted God's vision and dream,
    Moses 'saw' God in a burning bush,
Hannah prayed, got Samuel and thanked God,
    The priest thought she was a lush.
Saul, David, Solomon were led by their Lord.
    New Testament visions were through God's Angel;
    Mary saw vision and blessing through Gabriel,
Shepherds, wise men, saw Angel host,
    Joseph fled with Angel to Egypt and lived.
Jesus was filled with His Father's Holy Ghost,
    Jesus spoke to Father God as in the cross He bled,
Jesus died, rose and ascended to heaven with Father.
Jesus talks to us, His followers, who gather,
    Love God, love neighbor is His advice.
    God's communication to live well for us suffice.
So talk to God, pray unceasing, sin confessing,
With thanks be to God for abundant blessing.
    With all benediction common, rare and dear,
    Lord in your mercy, hear our prayer.

My Footprints (in the sand)

Adam kicked out of Eden through original sin;
Abel murdered; God found out and marked Cain.
    Noah built an ark from floods to survive;
    Abraham sent to foreign lands to multiply and live.
Isaac, Jacob, Joseph led by God as Israel in Egypt;
Moses wandered with his people through God's promises kept.
    Sages, prophets to Kings Saul, David and Solomon;
    Taken to lands and destinations unknown.
Jesus in Gethsemane dragged to the cross;
Through God's footprints great ones got across.
    God guides me as His child in paths I cannot see;
    I kick and scream like a sinner, at things that cannot be.
But when I see one set of footprints in the sand,
I know God is carrying me across to His Holy Land.

God's Seasons

Ah, the changing colors of Fall,
    Green gives way to brighter colors.
Hockey puck replaces a baseball,
    Closed windows shut out neighbors,
Colder weather turns the heat on,
Warmer clothes as we all adorn.
    Put away the lawn mower,
    Get ready the snow blower,
Seasons change and Fall begin,
Setting up scary Halloween.
    Shorter days bring Devil's night,
Ghosts and goblins abound,
    One and other scare and fright,
Kids in costumes run around.
    Trick or treat; kids walk the beat,
    Kids gather bags with things sweet.
Colder days of November,
For Thanksgiving we all gather.
    Snowy days of December,
    White Christmas is not a bother.
As long as the winter blues,
Gives way to Spring green hues.
    Four seasons we endure,
    Each a different pleasure.
Winter, spring, summer or fall,
All we have to do is have a ball.
    Year to year as we this repeat,
    It is time for us to one and other greet.
New Year, Easter, Thanksgiving or Christmas,
Happy Seasons, God does bless.

FAITH

Life's best instructions are in the BIBLE.
Makes our life on earth livable.
    Take it literal or with a grain of salt,
    Better life with evil put to a halt.
Faith as big as a mustard seed,
Good enough to accomplish many a deed.
    Move a mountain, cure a human,
    God's gift to us is given.
Faith is the first step to take,
On a tough road for us to evil break.
    All talent given to us to serve,
    Increases the faith we deserve.
Faith in Father, Son and Holy Ghost,
For us to reach God, the heavenly host.

BIBLE Myths

Many myths abound about the Holy BIBLE.
Yet it never takes away from making life livable.
    God made and named Adam who named Eve,
    Serpent gave 'fruit'; not Apple as we believe.
Moses did ask God directions to the Promised Land.
Jonah was inside 'A big fish', but not in a whale found.
    Noah flood, Babel, Sod'om & Go-mor'rah,
    Abraham seed in new land thru wife Sarah.
Saul, David, Solomon – all ruled Israel well.
Through Prophets God spoke & led Israel to dwell.
    Wise men visited Jesus by following a star,
    'Three kings' is a myth per their gold, frankincense and myrrh.
Though God is everywhere, He used Angels.
BIBLE instructions are no myth for humans.
    Though Jesus never called Himself almighty God,
    Through Father, Son and Holy Ghost, He is our Savior Lord.

Epilogue Poem

Shepherd King David said;
   "Let the meditations of my heart be
Acceptable in thy sight Oh Lord
   My strength and my Redeemer" to me.
Let a few of my poems,
Holy prose set to rhyme,
   Be dedicated to thy sight.
   As evil and division we fight,
Dear Lord through your holy Son,
Save our lives and our sin.
   Bless these idle words to use,
   So we may pay for our earthly dues.
Searching for eternal wisdom,
To reach your heavenly Kingdom.

"Thanks Be To God For His Unspeakable Gift"
II Corinthians, Verse 15

C. R. Prabakaran
2014